World Art

Sue Nicholson

MINNETONKA, MINNESOTA

This edition published in 2006 in North America by
Two-Can Publishing
11571 K-Tel Drive
Minnetonka, MN 55343
www.two-canpublishing.com

Two-Can wishes to thank artist Shannon Steven for
her help with the American terms in this book.

Library of Congress CIP data on file

ISBN 1-58728-536-3

Written by Sue Nicholson
Designed by Caroline Grimshaw
Edited by Sian Morgan and Matthew Harvey
Projects made by Sarah Morley
Calligraphy by Ch'en-Ling
With thanks to Victoria, Sam, and Nicola

Creative Director: Louise Morley
Editorial Manager: Jean Coppendale

Picture Credits:

The Art Archive 6t, 8t, 8c, 10t & b, 14t & b, 24,26;
Corbis/Christie's Images 18t /Robert Holmes 17tc /Dave
G Houser 12 /Reza Webistan 22r / 28r
Royal Ontario Museum 18b /Dinodia 16, 17tl & c; **Japan
National Tourist Organization** 20

Printed and bound in China

1 2 3 4 5 10 09 08 07 06

The words in **bold** are
explained in the glossary
on page 30.

Contents

Tools and materials

On this page you can see some of the things you will need to do the projects in this book. Before you begin any of the activities, check to make sure you have everything you need.

1 Clear tape or masking tape
2 White glue
3 Dish of wallpaper paste for papier-mâché projects
4 Balloons
5 Paintbrushes
6 Brass fasteners
7 Poster paints
8 Air-drying modeling clay
9 Enamel paint
10 Beads, stick-on gems, and sequins
11 Colored paper
12 Paint roller
13 Crayons and colored chalk
14 Pencils
15 Ruler
16 Scissors
17 String
18 Tissue paper
19 Sketch pad
20 Cutting board

Paints and paintbrushes

As well as different colored poster paint, you will need some white **latex** paint for first coats on clay or papier-mâché models. You also need a selection of paintbrushes: a small brush from a hardware store (for glue or for painting large areas), a medium brush, and a thin brush for fine detail.

Sketchbook

Keep a sketchbook. Look for ideas in travel guides, books, and magazines about geography and history. Visit museums and sketch arts and crafts from different places countries and at different times in history.

Ancient world art

Many thousands of years ago in the **Stone Age**, people produced some amazing paintings. Many were made in caves—possibly as decorations for ceremonies or religious **shrines**. Follow the simple steps below to recreate a magical Stone-Age animal painting.

WHAT YOU NEED

- Air-drying modeling clay
- Rolling pin
- Sand
- Poster paint
- Black charcoal (optional)
- Cotton balls
- Sandpaper
- **Varnish** (optional)

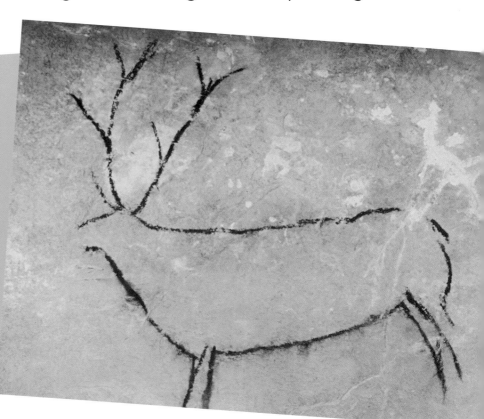

A Stone-Age cave painting

1 Lightly draw the outline of an animal, such as a cow, a deer, a bison, or an elephant, on scrap paper. Use a soft pencil and keep the lines simple.

TIP

Draw the animal's legs at an angle, not straight down, so it looks as though it is running.

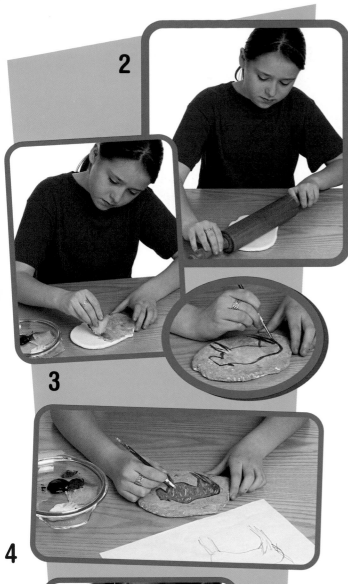

2 Roll out a piece of pale modeling clay the size of a tennis ball. It doesn't have to be totally smooth. Rub some sand over the clay to give the surface a rough texture. Then let the clay dry hard.

3 Use black and white paint to make a light gray. With cotton balls or a piece of foam, dab paint onto the clay to make it look like stone. When the surface is dry, paint a black outline of your animal.

TIP

You can seal your painting with varnish, or with a mixture of white glue and water. Put some white glue in a plastic cup. Gradually add water until it is the thickness of cream. It looks white when you paint it on, but it dries clear.

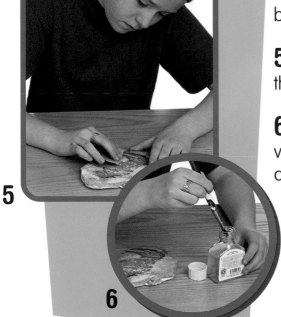

4 Paint the body in natural colors, such as dark browns and reds.

5 When the paint is dry, gently rub sandpaper over the surface to make the painting look patchy and old.

6 Add two coats of clear varnish. Let the varnish dry between coats.

African mask

Masks are used in many traditional African ceremonies. Some masks stand for animals or spirits. They may be made of wood, with shells, beads, fabric, or animal skins decorating them. Here's how to make your own African-style mask.

WHAT YOU NEED

- Pear-shaped balloon
- Newspaper
- Wallpaper paste
- Cardboard
- Masking tape
- White glue
- Poster paints
- Beads, shells, buttons, sequins, raffia, and string

African ceremonial masks

1 Blow up a balloon to the size of your head. Knot the end.

2 Follow the instructions on the package to make some wallpaper paste.

8

3 Soak newspaper strips (1 inch wide by 2 inches long) in the paste. Lay the strips neatly onto the balloon so they overlap. Add another layer of paper strips and let it dry. Repeat until you have eight layers.

3

4 When the paste is completely dry, pop the balloon with a pin. Have an adult help you trim the paper to make a mask shape. Cut out two holes for the eyes.

4

TIP
Tear, rather than cut, the newspaper. Torn edges lie flatter and overlap more easily.

5 Soak small pieces of paper in water until they break up into little pieces. Mash the paper with a fork, drain off the water, and squeeze it until it's almost dry. Mix the pulp with watered-down glue. Use it to build up eyebrows, a nose, and a mouth.

5

6 When the glue is dry, paint your mask a wood color. Highlight the features in dark brown, red, and gold paint. Decorate the mask with shells, beads, or buttons. Add hair using raffia, yarn, or string.

6

9

Egyptian amulet

Ancient Egyptians believed that a person's spirit needed to re-join its body after death in order to live forever. So people would decorate dead bodies with lucky charms called amulets to protect them on the hard journey. This Wedjat-eye charm warded off evil spirits.

WHAT YOU NEED

- Air-drying modeling clay
- Rolling pin or bottle
- Plastic knife
- Wooden or plastic modeling tools
- Poster paint
- Varnish

1 Roll out a piece of clay until it is ½ to ¾ inch thick and about ¾ inch larger than you want your finished eye to be. Carve the outline of an eye on the clay with a modeling tool or a pencil. Cut out the shape with a plastic knife.

Ancient Egyptian scarab (beetle) amulets

2 Roll out long, thin pieces of clay and press them into the eye shape to build up the design.

3 Use your tools to make patterns in the clay for decoration. Let the clay dry.

TIP

Everyday household objects such as a fork, a blunt nail, or the end of a paintbrush make great tools.

4 Paint the amulet in bright, rich colors. When the paint is dry, brush the surface with varnish. Let the first coat dry, then give it a second coat. Watch out, evil spirits!

TIP

To give the clay a smooth surface for decorating, you may wish to paint an undercoat of white **latex** paint. Let this dry before beginning step 4.

Ancient Greek vase

The best pottery in **Ancient Greece** was made in **Athens**. A vase like the one below would have stored oil, wine, or water. The vase in this project is made of papier-mâché, so don't put liquid in it!

1 Blow up the balloon. Make some wallpaper paste. Tear sheets of newspaper into strips about 1 inch wide and 2 inches long.

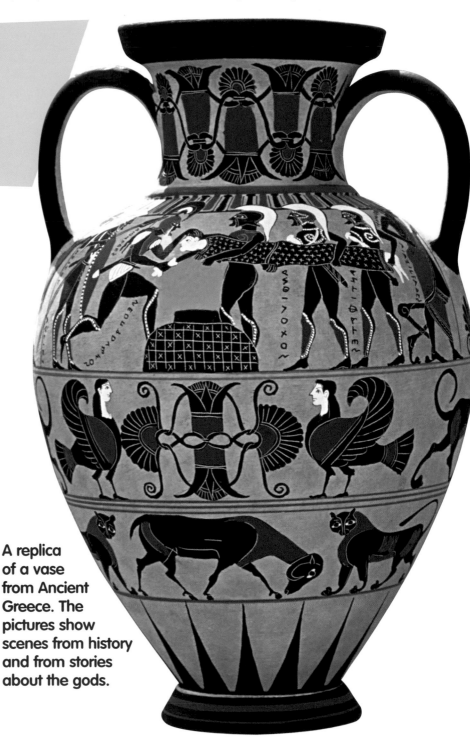

A replica of a vase from Ancient Greece. The pictures show scenes from history and from stories about the gods.

2 Soak the strips in the paste, then lay them over the balloon neatly so they overlap. Cover the balloon in two layers. Let it dry.

3 Repeat until you have eight layers. When the paste is dry, pop the balloon with a pin.

4 Cut out a strip of thin cardboard and tape the ends to make a ring about the same size as the bottom of the balloon. Tape the ring to the base of the balloon so that it stands up. Make a wider ring for the top. Cut two more strips of cardboard and tape them to the sides for handles.

5 Cover the cardboard base, top, and handles with two layers of papier-mâché. Make sure that the strips overlap the main part of the vase. When dry, add another layer.

6 When this is dry, paint the vase. We chose reddish brown for the middle and black for the base, rim, and handles.

7 Paint pictures and decorative borders on your vase. This one shows an owl—the symbol of the goddess **Athena**. When the paint is dry, varnish the whole thing.

Roman-style mosaic

The floors in many **Roman** homes contained a mosaic—a picture made of tiny glass, stone, or tile squares called tesserae. These mosaics often showed pictures of the gods or scenes from history.

WHAT YOU NEED

- Graph paper and a pencil
- Black construction paper
- Colored paper; or white paper and poster paints; or old magazines; or gummed colored paper
- Scissors
- White glue

1 Plan your design on graph paper, so the finished design is about 9 x 6 inches. It could be an animal, your initials, or just about anything! Design a border to frame your design.

Roman mosaics

2 Place the paper with the design on it face-down on the black construction paper. Rub the paper with the pencil, so the design transfers onto the paper.

3 Cut equal-size squares from the colors of paper you want to use in your mosaic.

TIP
- Squares cut from magazine photos give you different **hues** of each color, which will give your design more depth.
- Organize the squares before you start so similar colors are together.

4 Glue the squares onto the construction paper according to your design. Leave a gap about ⅛ inch wide around each square. You may need to cut some irregular shapes to fill in gaps in the picture.

5 To make your mosaic shine, paint it with white glue mixed with water.

TIP
If you want your mosaic to sparkle, cover some squares in glitter glue or paint them in gold or silver metallic paint.

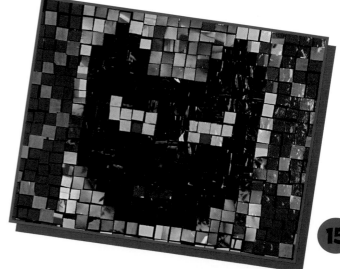

Indian Rangoli

Rangoli is the Indian art of decorating the floor or a wall with a **geometric** design, flowers, or animals. Intricate Rangoli are painted during **Hindu** festivals, such as **Diwali**, or for birthdays. Each state of India has its own style of Rangoli.

WHAT YOU NEED
- Sketch paper
- Pencil
- White chalk
- Colored chalk, or flour with food coloring

1 Practice drawing small shapes on sketch paper. When you're happy with a design, take a big sheet of paper and draw a series of evenly spaced dots.

An Indian woman making a Rangoli

2 Join dots to form a geometric pattern, a flower, or animal shape. Here are some ideas.

3 Copy your design onto the sidewalk or playground in chalk or in a flour–and–water paste (always ask permission first). You can also draw your Rangoli on a large sheet of black construction paper.

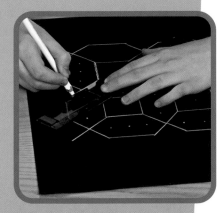

4 Fill in your Rangoli with chalk. If you are using flour paste, divide the paste into separate bowls and add a couple of drops of food coloring to each bowl.

TIP

Make sure your dots are evenly spaced so that you end up with a regular pattern.

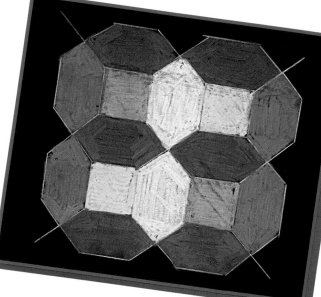

Chinese calligraphy

In China and Japan, calligraphy (beautiful writing produced with a brush) is an art form. Calligraphers spend months practicing one character, or symbol. This project will show you show to make the Chinese character for "Peace."

WHAT YOU NEED

- Paintbrush and paint (optional)
- Pencil
- Black marker
- White heavyweight paper
- Cream heavyweight paper
- Dark heavyweight paper
- Red marker
- Ruler
- Scissors

1 Draw the outline of the "Peace" character as shown below, using the graph lines to help you. If you are using a brush, follow the red arrows inside the outlines. Be patient!

Chinese calligraphy scroll

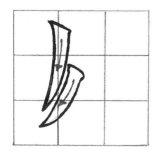

2 When you have completed the outlines, fill them in with a black marker. Try to keep within your pencil marks.

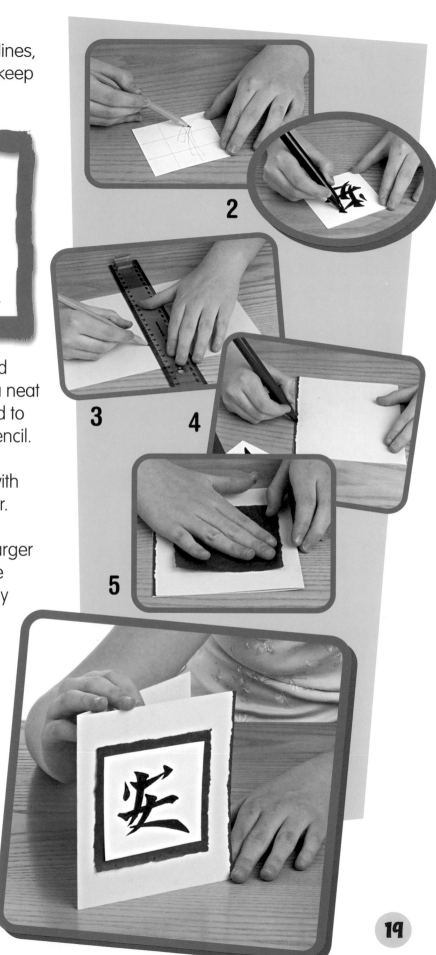

2

TIP

If you are using paint, try brushes of different sizes. A thick, pointed brush makes bold, sweeping strokes. Lift the brush away from the paper to make thin, light lines.

3

4

5

3 Cut out a rectangle of thick, textured cream paper. Fold it in half. To make a neat fold, measure where you want the fold to be with a ruler and mark the line in pencil.

4 Color the right edge of the paper with bright red poster paint or a red marker.

5 Cut a piece of dark paper slightly larger than your calligraphy and glue it to the cream paper. Now glue the calligraphy on top, so that a border of dark paper shows on all sides.

Here are two other Chinese characters to practice. They mean "Beautiful" (left) and "Lucky" (right).

Japanese banner

In Japan, on Children's Day, children hang up fish-shaped wind socks outside their homes to bring them good luck. Here's how to make your own fish to hang up in your room or classroom.

WHAT YOU NEED
- Colored tissue paper
- Glue
- Scissors
- Thin cardboard

1 Cut three shapes out of tissue paper, copying the shapes in the picture below. Choose a different color for each. The fish will fold along the center, so make sure the pieces are big enough.

Japanese fish banners

2 Glue the tail onto one end of the long section, and the head onto the other end.

3 Use your scissors to cut out lots of semicircles of tissue paper for the scales of the fish.

4 Cut out four large circles and two smaller circles to make the eyes. Glue them to the head of the fish.

TIP

When cutting out the scales, layer the tissue paper so you can cut lots of scales at once.

5 When you have enough scales, add them to the long section of the fish. Glue them from the tail upwards, and slightly overlap each row onto the previous one—just like real fish scales.

6 Measure the width of the head and cut a strip of cardboard the same length. Glue the ends to make a ring. Fold the fish down the center and glue the bottom edge. Glue the ring inside the mouth.

Indonesian puppets

Shadow puppets are one of the world's oldest storytelling traditions. Indonesian shadow puppets called Wayang Kulit have been popular entertainment in Indonesia for more than a thousand years. Here's how to make your own.

WHAT YOU NEED

- Paper
- Cardboard
- Pencil
- Scissors and craft knife
- Brass fasteners
- Wooden dowels or skewers
- Adhesive tape
- White sheet with any wrinkles ironed out
- Electric light

1 Sketch your puppet design roughly on paper. Give it a long nose, long, curling hair, a curving body, and bendy legs.

An Indonesian shadow puppet show

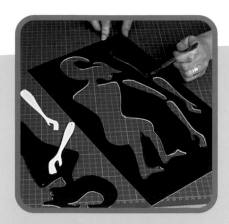

2 When you are happy with your design, draw the figure on cardboard. Draw the arms separately and divide each arm into two parts—shoulder to elbow, and elbow to hand. Round off the ends and cut out all the pieces. Ask an adult for help with the craft knife.

6 To put on a show, hang a thin white cotton sheet across a doorway or between two tall chairs. Shine an electric light onto the back of the sheet. Kneel down between the light and the sheet. Work the puppet above your head so that your audience sees the puppet's shadow. Use one hand to operate one arm, and the other hand to operate the other arm and the head.

3 Tape a long stick from the puppet's head down its back and behind one of its legs. Leave plenty of extra at the bottom for you to hold onto.

5 Tape a thin stick to each of the puppet's hands so you can move its arms.

4 Join the arms to the body at the shoulder with brass fasteners. Join the lower and upper parts of the arms at the elbow.

Stained glass

Stained-glass windows decorated churches and cathedrals in **medieval** times, and still do today. Make your own window, which glows in the light.

WHAT YOU NEED

- Black construction paper
- White pencil
- Craft knife and cutting board
- Scissors
- Colored tissue paper or colored cellophane
- Glue
- Fine black felt-tip pen

1 Plan your picture first. Keep it simple, with bold lines, and leave a 1- to 2-inch border around it for the frame. Then lightly draw your design on black construction paper with a white pencil. Leave a gap of ¼ to ½ inch between the different colors.

A medieval stained-glass window

BE CAREFUL!

You will need an adult to help you with this project.

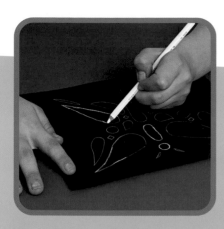

2 Once you are happy with your design, go over the lines again, this time marking them with bold, white **outlines**.

3 Ask an adult to help you cut out your design with a craft knife. Use a cutting board or several layers of cardboard.

4 Cut tissue paper or cellophane to fit over each opening in the paper. Put the pieces in place without glue first to check that they will fit over the holes.

6 Hold the window up to the light. The light will shine through the cellophane, making the colors glow.

5 Glue each piece to the back of the paper. Put glue around each hole, and try to keep glue off the front of the window.

TIP

As you cut more holes in the paper, the frame becomes more fragile. Keep a heavy book over the frame so it does not rip while you cut out the remaining pieces.

Arabian tile

Patterned tiles are a prized art form in **Islamic** countries such as Saudi Arabia. In this project, you can make a stencil, then use it to decorate a plain, white tile.

WHAT YOU NEED

- stiff, thin cardboard, 5½ x 5½ inches
- Craft knife and cutting board
- Masking tape
- Sponge or roller
- Ceramic paint (oil-based or water-based)
- Turpentine (for oil-based ceramic paints)
- Plain white tile, 6 x 6 inches
- Felt

Islamic tiles with geometric shapes and calligraphy

1 Plan out a tile design and practice drawing it. When you are happy with it, draw it onto the piece of cardboard.

BE CAREFUL!

You will need an adult to help you with this project.

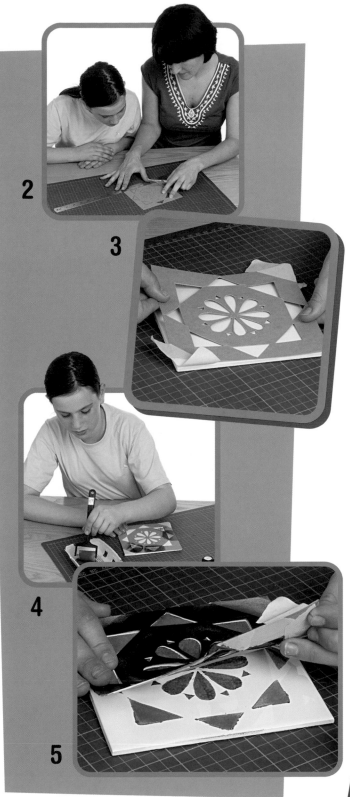

2 Ask an adult to help you cut around the lines with a craft knife. Use a cutting board.

3 Tape the edges of your cardboard stencil to a plain, white ceramic tile.

4 Dab ceramic paint onto the tile through the stencil with a small sponge, brush, or roller. Try to fill all the gaps with paint.

TIP

If you use oil-based paint, clean your brushes in turpentine. A cotton swab dipped in turpentine will wipe away mistakes.

5 Remove the stencil. If you used oil-based paint, let it dry. If it is water-based, ask an adult to help you to fire it in the oven, following the instructions on the paints.

6 Cut out a square of felt. Glue it to the back of your tile so you can put it on a table without scratching it.

Russian egg

The first Fabergé egg was made in 1885, when the Russian **Tsar**, Alexander III, commissioned a jeweled Easter egg for his wife from a **goldsmith** named Carl Fabergé. Here's how to "blow" a real egg and decorate it in the style of a fabulous Fabergé egg.

WHAT YOU NEED

- Raw egg
- Pin
- Bowl
- Enamel paints
- Dried lentils, peas, or beans
- Stick-on gems

1 Use a pin to poke a small hole in the top and the bottom of the egg.

The original Fabergé eggs were made of enamel and decorated with metals, such as silver, gold, and copper, and precious stones.

2 Hold the egg over a bowl and gently blow through one of the holes. The contents of the egg will dribble out until the egg is empty.

3 Holding the egg gently, paint the shell.

TIP
Use tweezers to pick up tiny seeds or gems, dip them in glue (or paint a layer of white glue on the egg first with a brush), and then drop them into place.

4 Decorate the egg using lentils, seeds, or stick-on gems for jewels. You can spray-paint the lentils first with gold or silver metallic paint. (If you do this, wear a mask and apron and protect your work surfaces.)

5 To make a stand for your egg, make a small ring out of thin cardboard and decorate it with paint and gems.

Glossary

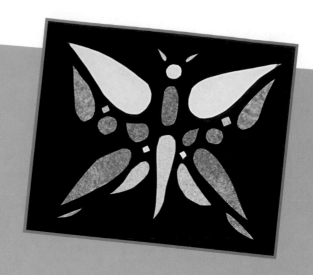

Ancient Egyptians the people of Ancient Egypt, the civilization that built the pyramids about 4,000 years ago

Ancient Greece a civilization dating back over 2,500 years, in which many new ideas about science and the arts were developed

Athena the Ancient Greek goddess of wisdom, represented by an owl

Athens the capital of Ancient Greece

Diwali an important Hindu or Sikh festival, held during October or November

geometric a pattern made up of regular shapes

goldsmith a person who makes objects out of gold

Hindu relating to Hinduism, one of India's main religions

hues different versions of the same basic color, such as lime green, kelly green, and forest green

Islamic relating to Islam, one of the world's major religions

latex a kind of paint used to paint walls

medieval relating to the period of history in Europe called the Middle Ages, between the years 500 to 1500

outlines lines that form the outer edge of something

Romans the people of Ancient Rome, a civilization that was centered in what is now Rome, Italy, around 2,000 years ago.

shrines holy places where people come to pray

Stone Age very early period of history when humans first used stone tools

tsar the Russian word for emperor

varnish clear paint that dries hard and protects and the surface beneath it

Index

Notes for parents and teachers

The projects in this book can be used as stand-alone art projects or as part of other areas of study, such as history or geography. The ideas in the book offer children inspiration, but you should always encourage them to draw from their own imagination and first-hand observation.

Sourcing ideas

All art projects should tap into children's interests and be relevant to their lives and experiences. Some stimulating starting points include books, magazines, travel guides, cultural websites, and museums. This will increase their awareness of the purposes of art, craft, and design in different times and cultures.

Digital cameras are handy for recording reference materials (museum exhibits, buildings, etc.) that can be printed out to look at during a project.

Other lessons can be an ideal springboard for an art project. A trip to a historical museum, a workshop on African music, or a story from another country all provide a wealth of ideas. Encourage children to talk about the types of art they have seen on family trips, at home, or at cultural festivals such as Chinese New Year or Diwali.

Encourage children to keep a sketchbook of their ideas, and to collect images and objects to help them develop their artwork.

Evaluating work

It's important and motivating for children to share their work with others, and to compare ideas and methods. Encourage them to talk about their work. What do they like best about it? How would they do it differently next time?

Show the children examples of artists' work from different periods and cultures. How did they approach similar subjects and problems? Do the children like the work? Why or why not?

Help children to recognize the originality and value of their work, to appreciate the different qualities in others' work, and to respect ways of working that are different from their own. Display children's work for all to admire!

Expanding the techniques

Look at ways to build on the projects—children could apply some of the techniques they have learned to make things from other countries. For example, adapt the papier-mâché African mask technique to make a South American carnival mask or a Venetian firebird mask. Similarly, children could look at the shape and style of shadow puppets in China and compare them with traditional Indonesian designs.

Discuss how stories have been created through art in different cultures and at different times—in cave paintings, paintings on Egyptian tombs, Greek vases, Chinese landscape paintings, or stained-glass windows. How would children represent their own stories—through sculpture, painting, masks, or puppetry?

Create a large world map for the classroom wall. Attach digital photographs of finished artwork to the countries from which the art originated. Find photographs in books, magazines, or travel brochures of other art from those countries and add them to the map as reference material.

Help your artist(s) set up an art gallery to show off their work, or scan artwork and post the images to a photo website where others can log in and view them. Having their work displayed professionally will make them feel that their work is valued.